Chefs' Special

Punjabi Kitchen

Chefs' Special

Punjabi Kitchen

Compiled by Master Chefs of India

Lustre Press
Roli Books

Flavours of Punjab

Punjab, the granary of the nation, is a green vision of swaying wheat and maize fields. Nestling at the foothills of the Himalaya, it is called the valley of the five rivers: the Beas, the Jhelum, the Sutlej, the Ravi and the Chenab. Punjab produces the bulk of India's wheat, which is of superlative quality.

The Punjabis are a vigorous people, fond of eating, working and merrymaking. They are robust people with robust appetites. Their mornings begin with thick parathas stuffed with vegetables, eaten with butter or spicy *chana* (chickpeas) cooked in a spicy and fragrant curry. A huge glass of creamy *lassi* (a yoghurt drink) washes down hot *jalebis* (fried gram flour roundels) dripping with sugar syrup.

Punjabi tandoori cooking is one of the most popular cuisines in the world. Huge earthen ovens called tandoors, half-buried in the ground, are made red hot with coal fire at the bottom. Marinated meat, chicken, fish, *paneer* (cottage cheese) and *rotis* (unleavened wholewheat breads) and *naans* (flat breads) of different types are cooked in the tandoor and the results are absolutely scrumptious! Today, most five-star hotels in India, and reputed Indian restaurants around the world, have tandoori kebabs, tandoori prawns and assorted tandoori breads on their menus. Punjabi mutton or chicken *kormas*, a Mughal legacy, are also immensely popular.

Punjab's winter is characterised by its golden mustard fields. It is during this season that Punjabis eat their national delicacy – steaming bowls of spicy *sarson ka saag* (mustard greens) topped with melting blobs of fresh butter served with *makkai ki roti* (maize flour bread). Farm picnics around bonfires and sumptuous food on cold autumn nights are a salient feature of Punjabi life.

Holi and Baisakhi, both colourful festivals of dance and song, are celebrated with great gusto. Punjabi weddings are glittering, joyous occasions, with an abundance of food and drink.

Punjabi cuisine is not only delicious, but a visual and olfactory delight as well. Crisp, tangy, spicy and wholesome – take 100 gm of adventurous spirit, deep-fry in 10 tbsp of enthusiasm, season with a pinch of experimentation, and create your own Punjabi gourmet delight!

Basic Preparations

Garam masala powder: Take 18 gm black cumin seeds (*shahi jeera*), 18 gm cumin seeds (*sabut jeera*), 40 gm cloves (*laung*), 12 bay leaves (*tej patta*), 40 black cardamom (*bari elaichi*) seeds, 6 cinnamon (*dalchini*) sticks, 25 black peppercorns (*sabut kali mirch*), 1 gm mace (*javitri*) and 9 gm dry ginger (*sonth*) powder.

Dry roast all the ingredients (except mace and dry ginger powder) on a low heat until aromatic. Remove from the heat and cool. Mix all the roasted spices, mace and dry ginger powder and grind to a fine powder. Sieve, and store in an airtight container.

Clarified butter (*ghee*): Heat some unsalted butter until it melts and froths. Remove the foam that rises on the top. Strain the melted butter into a heat-proof container. Discard the milk solids that are left behind. Let it cool at room temperature and then chill. When the chilled fat rises to the top, spoon it off, leaving the clarified butter behind.

Tomato purée: Peel and chop 8 tomatoes. Transfer them to a pan. Add 1 lt of water, 8 cloves (*laung*), 8 green cardamoms (*choti elaichi*), 15 gm ginger (*adrak*), 10 gm garlic (*lasan*), 5 bay leaves (*tej patta*) and 5 black peppercorns (*sabut kali mirch*). Cook on medium heat till the tomatoes are tender. Cool and purée in a blender. Use as per recipe.

Yoghurt (*dahi*): If you want to set yoghurt at home buy some starter from a sweet (*mithai*) shop. Heat 1 lt milk till it is warm to touch. Add 2 tsp of the starter (culture) to the milk and stir well. Transfer the mixture to a clay pot, cover with a lid and then keep in a warm place to ferment for 6-8 hours. In winter, it usually takes longer to set and also needs to be kept warmer than usual. In the summer months, it sets in a relatively short time.

Garlic-ginger (*lasan-adrak*) paste: Take equal amounts of garlic and ginger and soak overnight. Peel, chop and process in an electric blender with a small quantity of water. Blend at high speed to make a smooth paste. Remove and store in an airtight container and keep in the refrigerator for later use. The paste will keep for up to 4-6 weeks.

Saag Meat
Lamb cooked with spinach

Ingredients:

Lamb, cut into pieces	500 gm
Spinach (*palak*), chopped	4 cups / 300 gm
Clarified butter (*ghee*)	½ cup / 95 gm
Onions, chopped	1 cup / 240 gm
Ginger (*adrak*), paste	2 tsp / 12 gm
Garlic (*lasan*), paste	2 tsp / 12 gm
Coriander (*dhaniya*) powder	2 tsp / 3 gm
Red chilli powder	2 tsp / 3 gm
Turmeric (*haldi*) powder	1 tsp / 1½ gm
Cumin seeds (*sabut jeera*)	1 tsp / 2 gm
Garam masala powder (see p. 6)	1 tsp / 2 gm
Yoghurt (*dahi*)	½ cup / 90 gm
Salt	2 tsp / 9 gm

Method:

1. Heat the clarified butter in a wok (*kadhai*); stir in the onions and fry till light brown.
2. Add the ginger-garlic pastes and sauté for a while. Now, add the lamb and cook for 10 minutes.
3. Add the coriander powder, red chilli powder, turmeric powder, cumin seeds, garam masala powder, yoghurt and salt. Cook for 15 minutes.
4. Finally, add the spinach and cook on low heat till the spinach has wilted, the lamb is tender and there is hardly any liquid left.
5. Serve hot with a dash of clarified butter sprinkled on the top.

Lamb

Kadhai Gosht
Tender lamb in a thick gravy

Serves: 2-4

Ingredients:

Lamb, cut into ½" cubes	500 gm
For the marinade:	
Red chilli powder	1 tsp / 1½ gm
Cumin (*jeera*) powder	1 tsp / 1½ gm
Coriander (*dhaniya*) powder	1 tsp / 1½ gm
Aniseed (*saunf*) powder	2 tsp / 3 gm
Fenugreek (*methi*) leaves, fresh	2 tsp / 2 gm
Yoghurt (*dahi*)	1 cup / 180 gm
Oil	4 tbsp / 40 ml
Onion, large, chopped	1
Bay leaves (*tej patta*)	2
Cinnamon (*dalchini*), 2" stick	1
Cloves (*laung*)	6
Green cardamoms (*choti elaichi*)	6
Ginger (*adrak*), finely chopped	1 tsp / 3 gm
Garlic (*lasan*), finely chopped	1½ tsp / 3 gm
Salt to taste	

Method:

1. In a big bowl, combine all the ingredients for the marinade. Add the lamb, mix well and set aside to marinate for half an hour.
2. Heat the oil in a wok (*kadhai*); add the onion and sauté till translucent. Add the bay leaves, cinnamon stick, cloves, green cardamoms, ginger and garlic. Stir thoroughly and fry for 2-3 minutes.
3. Add the marinated lamb and salt. Mix well. Pour 1 cup of water and cook till the lamb is tender and the gravy is thick. Serve hot.

Rara Meat
Spicy lamb

Serves: 4-6

Ingredients:

Lamb, pieces	1 kg
Clarified butter (*ghee*)	1 cup / 190 gm
Onions, paste	1½ cups / 450 gm
Ginger (*adrak*), paste	4 tsp / 25 gm
Garlic (*lasan*), paste	4 tsp / 25 gm
Cinnamon (*dalchini*), 1" stick	1
Cloves (*laung*)	3
Tomato purée	1 cup / 200 ml
Red chilli powder	4 tsp / 6 gm
Turmeric (*haldi*) powder	1 tsp / 1½ gm
Coriander (*dhaniya*) powder	3 tsp / 4½ gm
Nutmeg (*jaiphal*), ground	½
Mace (*javitri*), ground	1 tsp / 1½ gm
Yoghurt (*dahi*)	1 cup / 180 gm

Salt to taste
Garam masala powder (see p. 6) 2 tsp / 4 gm
Green coriander (*hara dhaniya*),
  finely chopped   ½ cup / 12 gm

Method:

1. Heat the clarified butter in a wok (*kadhai*) over a medium-high flame. When hot, add the onion paste and fry till it turns light brown in colour.
2. Add the ginger-garlic pastes and sauté for a few seconds.
3. Add the cinnamon stick, cloves and the lamb. Cook till the lamb is slightly tender and brown.
4. Add the tomato purée, red chilli powder, turmeric

Lamb

powder, coriander powder, nutmeg, mace, yoghurt and salt. Cook for 10 minutes more on a medium flame.

5. Add the garam masala and 3 cups of water. Cook covered on low heat until the oil separates from the spices and comes to the surface.

6. The lamb should be quite tender by now. Remove the cover and let it simmer for 5-6 minutes, until enough of the liquid has evaporated, leaving a thick gravy.

7. Serve hot, garnished with green coriander.

Yoghurt Power

Add half a cup of yoghurt to chopped onions before frying them.
Yoghurt improves the taste and flavour of the dish.
It is also a handy substitute for tomatoes.

Raan Pathani
Spicy leg of lamb

Serves: 3-4

Ingredients:

Leg of lamb	1
For the marinade:	
Garlic (*lasan*), crushed	1 tsp / 6 gm
Ginger (*adrak*), crushed	1 tsp / 6 gm
Whole red chillies	
(*sabut lal mirch*), paste	1 tsp / 5 gm
Oil	1 tbsp / 10 ml
Grind to a paste:	
Onions, sliced	4-5
Garlic (*lasan*), crushed	1 tsp / 6 gm
Ginger (*adrak*), crushed	1 tsp / 6 gm
Whole red chillies	
(*sabut lal mirch*), paste	1 tsp / 5 gm
Coriander (*dhaniya*) powder	2 tsp / 3 gm
Cumin (*jeera*) powder	1 tsp / 2 gm
Turmeric (*haldi*) powder	¾ tsp / 1 gm
Oil	1 tbsp / 10 ml
Cloves	3
Green cardamoms (*choti elaichi*), crushed	4
Black cardamoms (*bari elaichi*), crushed	3
Cinnamon (*dalchini*), 2" sticks	2
Star anise (*chakri phool*)	2
Bay leaf (*tej patta*)	1
Tomato purée	6 tbsp / 120 ml
Salt	1 tsp / 4 gm

Method:

1. With a sharp knife, make deep incisions in the leg of lamb.
2. Combine all the ingredients for the marinade and

mix well. Cover the leg with this mixture and set aside to marinate for 3-4 hours.

3. Make a fine paste of all the ingredients mentioned with a little water. Keep aside.

4. Heat the oil in a wok (*kadhai*) that is large enough to hold the leg; sauté the cloves, green and black cardamoms, cinnamon sticks, star anise and bay leaf for 2-3 minutes. Add the ginger-garlic paste and fry until the oil separates from the spices and comes to the surface.

5. Add the tomato purée and salt. Fry for a few more minutes and then add the leg of lamb. Cook over low heat for about 2 hours or till the lamb is tender.

6. Before serving, grill the leg of lamb for a few minutes on both sides till brown.

Tender Meat

If the mutton is tough and cannot be cooked quickly, add a few pieces of betel-nut while cooking. This will help in softening the mutton.

Dal Gosht
Lamb cooked with Bengal gram

Serves: 6-8

Ingredients:

Lamb, cut into ½" cubes	1 kg
Bengal gram (*chana dal*), soaked for 2 hours	1½ cups / 240 gm
Oil	6 tbsp / 60 ml
Ginger-garlic (*adrak-lasan*) paste	4 tsp / 25 gm
Turmeric (*haldi*) powder	1 tsp / 1½ gm
Red chilli powder	2 tsp / 3 gm
Garam masala powder (see p. 6)	2 tsp / 4 gm
Onions, chopped, paste	3
Tomatoes, chopped, paste	4
Salt to taste	
Sugar	1 tsp / 3 gm
Yoghurt (*dahi*)	1 cup / 180 gm
Green coriander (*hara dhaniya*), finely chopped	1 tbsp / 5 gm

Method:

1. Drain and cook the Bengal gram in 1 cup water till tender, but not over cooked. Drain and keep aside.
2. Heat the oil in a wok (*kadhai*); add the lamb and fry till well browned. Add the ginger-garlic paste, turmeric powder, red chilli powder, garam masala powder and onion-tomato pastes. Reduce the heat and cook till the oil separates from the mixture.
3. Add the salt, sugar, yoghurt and 2½ cups of water. Cook on low heat till the lamb is tender. Add the Bengal gram and bring the mixture to a boil. Lower the heat and simmer until well blended.
4. Serve hot, garnished with green coriander.

Bhuna Gosht
Fried lamb

Lamb

Ingredients:

Lamb, cut into pieces	450 gm
Garlic (*lasan*), cloves	2 tsp / 12 gm
Ginger (*adrak*)	2 tsp / 12 gm
Red chilli powder	2 tsp / 3 gm
Turmeric (*haldi*) powder	¼ tsp
Oil	½ cup / 60 ml
Salt	1 tsp / 4 gm

Method:

1. Combine the garlic, ginger, red chilli powder and turmeric powder together and grind to a fine paste. Rub this paste into the lamb. Set aside to marinate for half an hour.
2. Heat the oil in a wok (*kadhai*); add the lamb and salt. Cover and cook on low heat for about 15 minutes or till the lamb is tender. Fry gently until it turns brown.
3. Serve hot.

Aab Gosht

Lamb curry cooked in milk

Ingredients:

Lamb, cut into pieces	1 kg
Water	5 cups / 1 lt
Aniseed (*saunf*) powder	5 tsp / 7½ gm
Garlic (*lasan*) cloves, crushed	5
Dry ginger powder (*sonth*)	1 tsp / 2 gm
Salt to taste	
Milk	5½ cups / 1 lt
Green caradmoms (*choti elaichi*), split open	6
Onion, paste, fried	1 tbsp / 25 gm
Black peppercorn (*kali mirch*) powder	1 tbsp / 6 gm
Clarified butter (*ghee*)	½ cup / 95 gm

Method:

1. Boil the lamb in water with the aniseed powder, garlic, dry ginger powder and salt till it is tender. Remove the lamb and keep aside. Sieve the stock in another pan and keep aside.
2. In a separate pan, boil the milk with the green cardamoms. Simmer till the milk is reduced to half. Add the fried onion paste, black peppercorn powder and clarified butter. Mix well.
3. Add the lamb and the stock. Stir well and bring the mixture to a boil. Continue to boil for 5-7 minutes and then reduce the heat to low and simmer for another 10 minutes.
4. Serve hot.

Kalegi Khara Masala

Liver cooked with tomatoes

Ingredients:

Liver (*kalegi*), finely sliced	450 gm
Butter	2 tbsp / 40 gm
Ginger (*adrak*), chopped	½"
Garlic (*lasan*) cloves, chopped	3
Spring onions (*hara pyaz*), finely chopped	5
Capsicum (*Shimla mirch*), deseeded, finely chopped	1
Green coriander (*hara dhaniya*), chopped	1 tbsp / 5 gm
Green chillies, chopped	3
Tomatoes, chopped	2
Salt	1 tsp / 4 gm
Black peppercorn (*kali mirch*) powder	¼ tsp

Method:

1. Heat the butter in a wok (*kadhai*); add the ginger, garlic and fry until light brown. Add the liver and fry for another 2 minutes.
2. Add the spring onions (keep aside a few for garnishing), capsicum, green coriander, green chillies and tomatoes. Mix well. Add the salt and black peppercorn powder. Fry till the tomato juice is absorbed and the liver is tender.
3. Serve hot, garnished with the remaining spring onions.

Lamb

Khasta Kalegi
Fried masala liver

Ingredients:

Liver (*kalegi*), thinly sliced	750 gm
For the marinade:	
Ginger (*adrak*) paste	2½ tsp / 15 gm
Garlic (*lasan*) paste	2½ tsp / 15 gm
Red chilli powder	2½ tsp / 4 gm
Black peppercorn (*kali mirch*) powder	1½ tsp / 3 gm
Salt to taste	
Lemon (*nimbu*) juice	1
Clarified butter (*ghee*)	½ cup / 95 gm

Method:

1. Marinate the liver with the ingredients mentioned for 1 hour.
2. In a large frying pan, heat the clarified butter. Add the marinated liver, a little at a time. Fry till crisp and tender. Remove with a slotted spoon and drain the excess oil on absorbent kitchen towels.
3. Serve hot.

Keema Mattar
Minced chicken with green peas

Serves: 2-4

Ingredients:

Chicken, minced	2½ cups
Green peas (*mattar*)	1½ cups
Butter	3 tbsp / 60 gm
Cumin seeds (*sabut jeera*)	1 tsp / 2 gm
Onions, chopped	1 cup / 240 gm
Garlic (*lasan*), crushed	2½ tbsp / 30 gm
Ginger (*adrak*), paste	2 tbsp / 36 gm
Whole red chillies (*sabut lal mirch*)	2
Salt to taste	
Tomato purée	3 tbsp / 45 ml
Green coriander (*hara dhaniya*), chopped	1 tbsp / 5 gm

Method:

1. Heat the butter in a wok (*kadhai*); add the cumin seeds and when they splutter add the onions and fry till light brown.
2. Add the minced chicken, garlic, ginger, whole red chillies, salt and tomato paste. Mix well and fry till the butter comes to the surface.
3. Add the green peas and cook till the peas turn soft and the mixture is dry and golden brown.
4. Serve hot, garnished with green coriander.

Tandoori Murgh
Grilled chicken

Serves: 4-6

Ingredients:

Chicken broilers	2 x 600 gm

For the first marinade:

Salt to taste	
Whole red chillies (*sabut lal mirch*), paste	5 tsp / 25 gm
Ginger (*adrak*), paste	2 tsp / 12 gm
Garlic (*lasan*), paste	3 tsp / 20 gm
Lemon (*nimbu*) juice	2 tbsp / 30 ml

For the second marinade:

Yoghurt (*dahi*)	1 cup / 180 gm
Cumin (*jeera*) powder	1 tsp / 3 gm
Garam masala powder (see p. 6)	2 tsp / 4 gm
Ginger (*adrak*), paste	5 tsp / 30 gm
Lemon (*nimbu*) juice	2 tbsp / 30 ml
Oil	3 tbsp / 30 ml
Whole red chillies (*sabut lal mirch*), paste	5 tsp / 25 gm
Saffron (*kesar*), soaked in 2 tbsp warm milk	a few strands
Salt to taste	

Clarified butter (*ghee*) for basting

Method:

1. Clean the chicken, remove the skin and make 3 incisions each on the breasts and thighs and 2 on each drumstick. Repeat the same procedure with the second chicken.

2. Combine all the ingredients for the first marinade and rub this paste over both the chickens. Keep aside for 10 minutes.
3. Whisk the yoghurt in a large bowl and add the remaining ingredients for the second marinade. Mix well.
4. Rub both the chickens with this mixture and set aside to marinate for 3½ hours.
5. Skewer each chicken and roast in a preheated oven at high heat for 15 minutes or until the chicken is tender.
6. Baste the chicken with the clarified butter and roast for another 3 minutes. Serve hot.

Selecting a Chicken
Don't buy a chicken with a yellow skin and flesh.
Buy one with white flesh and skin.

Murgh Makhani
Chicken in a rich butter gravy

Serves: 4-6

Ingredients:

Tandoori chickens, cooked, cut into pieces (see p. 24)	2 x 600 gm
Cinnamon (*dalchini*) sticks	2
Black cardamoms (*bari elaichi*), crushed	3
Green cardamoms (*choti elaichi*), crushed	3
Cloves (*laung*)	3
Bay leaves (*tej patta*)	2
Tomatoes, chopped	1 kg
Onions, chopped	2
Ginger (*adrak*), chopped	1"
Garlic (*lasan*) cloves, chopped	8-10
Green chillies, chopped	8
Butter	2½ cups / 425 gm
Red chilli powder	1 tsp / 1½ gm
Sugar	3 tsp / 12 gm
Salt	½ tsp / 2 gm
Cream	½ cup / 100 ml
Garam masala powder (see p. 6)	½ tsp / 1 gm
Capsicum (*Shimla mirch*), chopped	1

Method:

1. In a large pan, add the cinnamon sticks, black and green cardamoms, cloves, bay leaves, tomatoes, onions, ginger, garlic and green chillies. Cook until the tomatoes turn soft. Remove from the heat and keep aside to cool.

2. Purée this tomato mixture in a blender, then strain through a sieve to obtain a smooth sauce.

3. Heat the butter in a pan; add the tomato sauce, red chilli powder, sugar and salt. Bring the mixture to a boil and then simmer until thick.

4. Add half the cream and the tandoori chicken. Continue to simmer for another 5 minutes. Now add the remaining cream (keep 1 tbsp aside for garnishing) and half of the garam masala powder. Stir well. Add the capsicum and cook till it is soft.

5. Serve hot, sprinkled with 1 tbsp of cream and the remaining garam masala powder.

Instant Relief

When peeling garlic skin, your fingertips can burn from garlic juice. Application of toothpaste to the affected area will relieve the pain.

Murgh Kasoori

Chicken flavoured with fenugreek leaves

Serves: 4-6

Ingredients:

Chicken, boneless, cut into pieces	1 kg
Yoghurt (*dahi*), whisked	1¼ cups / 225 ml
Salt to taste	
Oil	¾ cup / 135 ml
Green cardamoms (*choti elaichi*)	10
Black cardamoms (*bari elaichi*)	2
Cloves (*laung*)	8
Cinnamon (*dalchini*) sticks	2
Bay leaves (*tej patta*)	2
Caraway seeds (*shahi jeera*)	½ tsp / 1 gm
Onion, chopped	1 tbsp / 12 gm
Garlic (*lasan*), chopped	6 tsp / 24 gm
Ginger (*adrak*), chopped	3½ tbsp / 85 gm
Green chillies, deseeded, chopped	3 tsp / 15 gm
Turmeric (*haldi*) powder	1 tsp / 1½ gm
Coriander (*dhaniya*) powder	1½ tsp / 2½ gm
Red chilli powder	2 tsp / 3 gm
Water	1¼ cups / 250 ml
Tomatoes, chopped	¾ cup / 150 gm
Dry fenugreek leaves (*kasoori methi*) or	3 tsp / 1½ gm
Fresh fenugreek leaves (*methi*)	1 cup
Mace (*javitri*), powder	1 tsp / 2 gm
Garam masala powder (see p. 6)	2 tsp / 4 gm
Ginger (*adrak*), julienned	2 tsp / 15 gm
Green coriander (*hara dhaniya*), chopped	1 tbsp / 5 gm

Chicken

Method:

1. Mix the chicken with the yoghurt and salt. Set aside to marinate for 30 minutes.
2. Heat the oil in a wok (*kadhai*); add the green and black cardamoms, cloves, cinnamon sticks and bay leaves. Sauté for a few minutes.
3. Add the caraway seeds and onions and fry until golden brown.
4. Add the garlic, ginger and green chillies and fry for a few more minutes. Now, add the turmeric, coriander and red chilli powders with 4 tbsp of water. Stir thoroughly.
5. Add the tomatoes and fry over low heat until the oil comes to the surface.
6. Add the marinated chicken and the remaining water. Bring to a boil, cover and simmer until the chicken is cooked. (In case fresh fenugreek is used, cook with the chicken.)
7. Stir in the dry fenugreek leaves, mace powder, garam masala and ginger. Cover and cook on a low flame for 5 minutes.
8. Serve hot, garnished with green coriander.

Amritsari Machchi
Crispy fried fish

Serves: 4-6

Ingredients:

Fish, fillets	1 kg
For the batter:	
Oil	1½ tbsp / 15 ml
Gram flour (*besan*)	1½ cups / 150 gm
Egg, lightly beaten	1
Garlic-ginger (*lasan-adrak*), crushed	½ tsp
Red chilli powder	½ tsp / 1½ gm
Carom seeds (*ajwain*)	1 tsp / 3 gm
Salt	1 tsp / 4 gm
Green coriander, chopped	1 tbsp / 5 gm
Green chillies, deseeded, chopped	1-2
Lemon (*nimbu*) juice	2 tsp / 10 ml

Oil for deep frying
Garam masala powder (see p. 6)   a pinch

Method:

1. Heat the oil in a wok (*kadhai*); add the gram flour. Stir continuously for 1 minute. Remove from the heat and keep aside to cool.
2. When cool, add the remaining ingredients for the batter.
3. Coat the fish fillets with this mixture and keep aside for 20 minutes.
4. Heat the oil and fry the fish until the batter is crisp and the fish is done. Remove with a slotted spoon and drain on absorbent kitchen towels.
5. Serve hot, sprinkled with garam masala powder.

Fish Tikka
Tangy grilled fish

Serves: 4-6

Ingredients:

Fish, cut into cubes	1 kg
For the first marinade:	
Salt to taste	
Lemon (*nimbu*) juice	1 tbsp / 15 ml
For the second marinade:	
Yoghurt (*dahi*)	½ cup / 90 gm
Vinegar (*sirka*)	1 tbsp / 15 ml
Garam masala powder (see p. 6)	1 tsp / 2 gm
Cumin (*jeera*) powder	2 tsp / 3 gm
Carom seeds (*ajwain*)	½ tsp
Red chilli powder	1 tsp / 1½ gm
Garlic (*lasan*), paste	2 tsp / 12 gm

Clarified butter (*ghee*) / oil for basting

Method:

1. Sprinkle salt and lemon juice on the fish cubes. Mix well and keep aside for 1 hour to marinate.
2. In a bowl, combine the ingredients for the second marinade. Mix and coat the fish cubes evenly with this mixture. Set aside to marinate for 1 hour.
3. Arrange the fish cubes under a preheated grill until half done.
4. Baste with clarified butter or oil and grill until tender. Serve hot.

Machli Tamatar Ka Salan

Tomato fish curry

Serves: 5-6

Ingredients:

Fish, cut into 1" x 2" pieces, cleaned	1 kg
Turmeric (*haldi*) powder	1 tsp / 1½ gm
Salt to taste	
Clarified butter (*ghee*)	½ cup / 95 gm
Onions, chopped	1 cup / 240 gm
Garlic (*lasan*) paste	3 tsp / 18 gm
Ginger (*adrak*) paste	3 tsp / 18 gm
Red chilli powder	2 tsp / 3 gm
Black peppercorn (*kali mirch*) powder	1 tsp / 2 gm
Tomatoes, large, chopped	2

Method:

1. Pat dry the fish; rub in the salt and turmeric powder. Keep aside to marinate for half an hour.
2. Heat the clarified butter in a large saucepan. When hot, add the onions. Sauté until translucent. Add the garlic-ginger pastes, red chilli and black peppercorn powders. Fry until light brown.
3. Add the fish and stir gently for 2-3 minutes. Add the tomatoes. Reduce the heat and cook uncovered till the tomatoes are soft and form a coarse pulp. Cook until the fish is tender and the gravy is thick.
4. Serve hot.

Jhinga Jalfrezi
Stir-fried prawns

Serves: 4-6

Ingredients:

Prawns (*jhinga*), deveined, cleaned	750 gm
Clarified butter (*ghee*)	½ cup / 95 gm
Whole red chillies (*sabut lal mirch*), crushed	6
Cumin seeds (*jeera*)	1½ tsp / 3 gm
Salt to taste	
Black peppercorn (*kali mirch*) powder	1½ tsp / 3 gm
Ginger (*adrak*), julienned	2 tsp / 16 gm
Tomato purée	½ cup / 100 ml
White vinegar (*sirka*)	1½ tbsp / 22 ml
Green coriander (*hara dhaniya*), chopped	½ tbsp / 2½ gm

Method:

1. Heat the clarified butter in a wok (*kadhai*); add the whole red chillies. Stir and add the cumin seeds. When they crackle, add the prawns, salt, black peppercorn powder and ginger. Stir well. Reduce the heat and cook covered until the prawns are almost tender.

2. Add the tomato purée and white vinegar. Cook until the prawns are completely done.

3. Serve hot, garnished with coriander leaves.

Jhinga Kari
Tangy prawn curry

Ingredients:

Prawns (*jhinga*), shelled, deveined	500 gm
Lemon (*nimbu*) juice	1 tbsp / 15 ml
Clarified butter (*ghee*)	1 tbsp / 15 ml
Tomatoes, quartered	3
Garlic (*lasan*) cloves	10
Ginger (*adrak*), julienned	2 tsp / 16 gm
Green chillies, slit	6
Red chilli powder	2 tsp / 3 gm
Turmeric (*haldi*) powder	1 tsp / 1½ gm
Cumin (*jeera*) powder	1 tsp / 1½ gm
Salt to taste	

Method:

1. Mix the prawns well with the lemon juice. Set aside for 10 minutes. Wash the prawns under running water. Drain and keep aside.
2. Heat the clarified butter in a wok (*kadhai*); add the tomatoes. Stir and add the garlic, ginger and green chillies. Sauté until the tomatoes turn soft.
3. Add ½ cup water and bring the mixture to a boil. Mix in the red chilli, turmeric and cumin powders. Add the salt and the prawns. Cook for 8-10 minutes until the water evaporates and the prawns are done.
4. Serve hot.

Arvi Ka Chaat

Tangy colocasia

Serves: 4-6

Ingredients:

Colocasia (*arvi*), boiled, cubed	500 gm
Salt	2 tsp / 9 gm
Tomatoes, chopped	½ cup / 100 gm
Lemon (*nimbu*) juice	3 tbsp / 45 ml
Green chillies, chopped	4
Green coriander (*hara dhaniya*), chopped	¼ cup / 6 gm
Mint leaves (*pudina*), chopped	a few
Dry mango powder (*amchur*)	2 tsp / 4 gm

Method:

1. Combine the salt, tomatoes, lemon juice, green chillies, green coriander and mint leaves in a bowl. Add the colocasia and mix well.
2. Sprinkle dry mango powder over the colocasia mixture and serve.

Paneer Pudina Tikka

Grilled cottage cheese flavoured with mint

Serves: 4-6

Vegetarian

Ingredients:

Cottage cheese (*paneer*), 1" cubes	800 gm
Red chilli powder	1 tsp / 1½ gm
Turmeric (*haldi*) powder	1 tsp / 1½ gm
Salt to taste	
Juice of lemons (*nimbu*)	10
Garam masala powder (see p. 6)	2 tsp / 4 gm

For the filling:

Mint leaves (*pudina*), chopped	5 tbsp / 20 gm
Green coriander (*hara dhaniya*), chopped	5 tbsp / 20 gm
Green chillies, chopped	5
Yoghurt (*dahi*)	1¼ cups / 225 gm
Ginger (*adrak*), chopped	1 tbsp / 25 gm
Ginger-garlic (*adrak-lasan*) paste	4 tbsp / 40 gm
Yellow chilli powder	5 tsp / 7½ gm
Carom seeds (*ajwain*)	2 tsp / 3 gm
White pepper (*safed mirch*) powder	1 tsp / 2 gm
Clarified butter (*ghee*)	4 tbsp / 60 gm

Method:

1. To the cottage cheese, add the red chilli powder, turmeric powder, salt, lemon juice and half the garam masala powder and mix well.
2. For the filling, mix all the ingredients in a bowl thoroughly.
3. Slit the cottage cheese from the centre and spread this filling carefully.
4. In a bowl, combine the yoghurt, ginger,

ginger-garlic paste, yellow chilli powder, carom seeds, white pepper powder and mix well. Coat the cottage cheese cubes evenly with this mixture.

5. Skewer the cottage cheese and grill until golden brown.
6. Sprinkle the remaining garam masala before serving.

Yoghurt Care
To prevent yoghurt from turning sour, add a piece of coconut to it.

Vegetable Samosas
Deep-fried vegetable patties

Serves: 4-6

Ingredients:

Refined flour (*maida*)	250 gm
Clarified butter (*ghee*)	½ cup / 95 gm
Carom seeds (*ajwain*)	½ tsp
Salt	½ tsp / 2 gm
For the filling:	
Oil	3 tbsp / 30 ml
Cumin seeds (*sabut jeera*)	½ tsp / 1 gm
Potatoes, boiled, finely diced	250 gm
Green peas (*mattar*), boiled	50 gm
Salt	½ tsp / 2 gm
Coriander (*dhaniya*) powder	1 tsp / 1½ gm
Turmeric (*haldi*) powder	½ tsp / 1 gm
Red chilli powder	1 tsp / 1½ gm
Green chillies, deseeded, finely chopped	10

Dry mango powder (*amchur*)   1 tsp / 2 gm

Oil for frying

Method:

1. Add the clarified butter to the refined flour and rub till the mixture is crumbly. Add the carom seeds and salt. Mix well. Add just a little water to make a firm but pliable dough. Cover the dough with a moist cloth and keep aside for half an hour.
2. Heat the oil in a wok (*kadhai*); add the cumin seeds. When they crackle, add the potatoes and green peas. Stir for a minute. Add the salt, coriander, turmeric, red chilli powders, green chillies and dry mango powder. Mix well and cook till the

vegetables are done. Keep the filling aside to cool.

3. Divide the dough equally into lemon-sized balls. Flatten each ball and roll out to make a thin 3″ disc. Repeat the same procedure with the remaining balls.

4. Put a spoonful of the filling in half of the disc. Fold the other half over enclosing the filling, pressing the edges firmly to seal.

5. Heat the oil in a wok (*kadhai*); deep-fry the patties until golden brown. Remove with a slotted spoon and drain on absorbent kitchen towels.

6. Serve hot with tomato sauce.

Insect-free Flour
*Insects will not attack refined flour (*maida)*
if you pack it in a polythene bag and
place it in the refrigerator.

Pakora
Vegetable fritters

Vegetarian

Ingredients:

Potato, large, peeled, sliced	1
Aubergine (*baingan*), small, sliced	1
Onion, large, sliced	1
For the batter:	
Gram flour (*besan*)	2 cups / 200 gm
Salt	1 tsp / 4 gm
Red chilli powder	1 tsp / 1½ gm
Baking powder	½ tsp / 3 gm

Oil for frying

Method:

1. In a bowl, combine all the ingredients for the batter. Mix well, adding a little water to make a very thick batter.
2. Heat the oil in a wok (*kadhai*); dip the sliced vegetables into the batter, one at a time, and deep-fry until crisp and golden brown. Remove with a slotted spoon and drain the excess oil on absorbent kitchen towels.
3. Serve hot with tomato sauce.

Sarson Ka Saag
Spicy mustard greens

Serves: 4-6

Ingredients:

Mustard greens (*sarson*),
    finely chopped   1 kg
Spinach (*palak*), finely
    chopped   3¼ cups / 250 gm
Maize flour (*makkai ka atta*),
    sieved at least 3 times   3 tbsp / 25 gm
Salt to taste
Clarified butter (*ghee*)   ½ cup / 95 gm
Ginger (*adrak*), chopped   3 tsp / 24 gm
Garlic (*lasan*) cloves, chopped   5
Green chillies, finely chopped   3
Whole red chillies (*sabut lal mirch*)   3

Method:

1. Boil the mustard greens and spinach in 4 cups of water until soft. Drain and blend to make a coarse paste.

2. Heat a pan and add the green paste. Pour in 1 cup of water. Cook, stirring and mashing the paste against the sides of the pan. Add the maize flour and salt and cook for at least 45 minutes, adding water as and when required.

3. Heat the clarified butter in a frying pan; add the ginger, garlic and green chillies. Sauté until they change colour. Add the whole red chillies. Fry for another 2 minutes. Pour in the green paste and cook on a low heat for 30 minutes.

4. Serve hot with *makkai ki roti* (see p. 83).

Methi Aloo
Fresh fenugreek leaves with potatoes

Serves: 2-4

Ingredients:

Fenugreek leaves (*methi*), fresh,
   chopped   1 kg
Potatoes, diced   ½ kg
Clarified butter (*ghee*)   4 tbsp / 60 gm
Whole red chillies (*sabut lal mirch*),
   roasted   6
Coriander seeds (*sabut dhaniya*)   2 tsp / 4 gm
Cumin seeds (*sabut jeera*)   1 tsp / 1½ gm
Ginger (*adrak*), julienned   2 tbsp / 36 gm
Garlic (*lasan*), julienned   2 tbsp / 36 gm
Asafoetida (*hing*)   a pinch
Salt to taste

Method:

1. Sprinkle a little salt over the fenugreek leaves and keep aside for half an hour.
2. Heat the clarified butter in a wok (*kadhai*); add the whole red chillies, coriander seeds, cumin seeds, ginger, garlic, asafoetida and salt. Sauté for a few minutes.
3. Add the potatoes and fenugreek leaves. Cook on low heat till the vegetables are tender and the mixture is dry.
4. Serve hot.

Gobi Aloo
Crispy cauliflower with potatoes

Ingredients:

Cauliflower (*phool gobi*), cut into florets	500 gm
Potatoes, washed, diced	500 gm
Clarified butter (*ghee*)	½ cup / 95 gm
Cumin seeds (*sabut jeera*)	1 tsp / 2 gm
Ginger (*adrak*), chopped	2 tbsp / 36 gm
Salt to taste	
Turmeric (*haldi*) powder	1 tsp / 1½ gm
Red chilli powder	2 tsp / 3 gm
Green chillies, chopped	5
Green coriander (*hara dhaniya*), chopped	½ cup / 12½ gm

Method:

1. Heat the clarified butter in wok (*kadhai*); add the cumin seeds and ginger. Sauté for a while.
2. Add the cauliflower and potatoes. Mix well. Add salt, turmeric powder, red chilli powder and green chillies. Cover the pan and cook on low heat for 15 minutes or till the vegetables are done.
3. Serve hot, garnished with green coriander.

Variya Aloo
Sun-dried dumplings with potatoes

Serves: 2-4

Ingredients:

Sun-dried dumplings (*variya*)	200 gm
Potatoes, washed, quartered	500 gm
Clarified butter (*ghee*)	½ cup / 95 gm
Onion, paste	1 cup / 300 gm
Ginger (*adrak*), paste	3 tsp / 18 gm
Garlic (*lasan*), paste	2 tsp / 12 gm
Tomato purée	1 cup / 200 ml
Coriander (*dhaniya*) powder	2 tsp / 3 gm
Turmeric (*haldi*) powder	1 tsp / 1½ gm
Red chilli powder	1 tsp / 1½ gm
Salt to taste	

Method:

1. Heat the clarified butter in a wok (*kadhai*); fry the sun-dried dumplings till light brown in colour. Remove and keep aside.
2. In the same clarified butter, add the onion, ginger and garlic pastes. Fry till light brown.
3. Add the tomato purée. Cook for a few minutes. Add the coriander, turmeric, red chilli powders, salt and 2 cups of water. Mix well.
4. To this mixture, add the sun-dried dumplings and potatoes and cook till they are soft and tender, and the gravy is thick.
5. Serve hot.

Bharva Bhindi
Stuffed okra

Vegetarian

Ingredients:

Okra (*bhindi*), washed, dried	500 gm
For the filling:	
Dry mango (*amchur*) powder	2 tbsp / 16 gm
Red chilli powder	1 tsp / 1½ gm
Turmeric (*haldi*) powder	1 tsp / 1½ gm
Coriander (*dhaniya*) powder	2 tbsp / 9 gm
Cumin (*jeera*) powder	1 tsp / 3 gm
Salt to taste	
Clarified butter (*ghee*)	2 tbsp / 30 gm

Method:

1. Slit each okra from the centre without cutting it into two halves.
2. For the filling, combine all the ingredients in a bowl and mix thoroughly.
3. Fill each okra with this mixture carefully.
4. Heat the clarified butter in a pan; add the stuffed okra gently and cook on low heat till done.
5. Serve hot.

Bharva Karela
Stuffed bitter gourd

Serves: 2-4

Ingredients:

Bitter gourd (*karela*), medium-sized, scraped	500 gm
Clarified butter (*ghee*)	3 tbsp / 45 gm
For the filling:	
Onion, paste	4 tbsp / 80 gm
Garlic (*lasan*), paste	4 tsp / 25 gm
Ginger (*adrak*), paste	4 tsp / 25 gm
Tomato purée	2 tbsp / 30 ml
Coriander (*dhaniya*) powder	2 tsp / 4 gm
Red chill powder	3 tsp / 4½ gm
Dry mango (*amchur*) powder	4 tsp / 8 gm
Cumin (*jeera*) powder	2 tsp / 3 gm
Turmeric (*haldi*) powder	2 tsp / 3 gm
Garam masala powder (see p. 6)	1 tsp / 2 gm
Salt to taste	

Method:

1. Boil the bitter gourd in 2 cups water with salt for 10 minutes. Drain, cool and slit open. Without separating the two halves remove the seeds.
2. Heat the clarified butter in a wok (*kadhai*); add the onion, garlic and ginger pastes. Fry till light brown. Add the remaining ingredients. Mix well and cook until all the water has evaporated.
3. Remove from the heat and let the filling cool. Then stuff this inside the bitter gourd and wrap white thread around them from one end to the other 5 or 6 times to seal the filling.
4. Heat 2 tbsp of oil in a frying pan; fry the bitter gourd on low heat until light brown.
5. Remove the threads and serve hot.

Tinda Ka Bharta

Mashed round gourd

Vegetarian

Ingredients:

Round gourd (*tinda*), medium-sized	
peeled, boiled, grated	500 gm
Clarified butter (*ghee*)	¾ cup / 130 gm
Onions, chopped	1 cup / 240 gm
Tomatoes, chopped	1 cup / 200 gm
Whole red chillies (*sabut lal mirch*)	3
Cumin seeds (*sabut jeera*),	
roasted	1 tsp / 2 gm
Red chilli powder	1 tsp / 1½ gm
Salt to taste	
Dry fenugreek leaves	
(*kasoori methi*)	1 tsp / ½ gm
Green chillies	5
Green coriander (*hara dhaniya*),	
chopped	2 tbsp / 8 gm

Method:

1. Heat the clarified butter in a wok (*kadhai*); add the onions and tomatoes and fry for a while.
2. Add the whole red chillies, cumin seeds, red chilli powder, salt, dry fenugreek leaves and mix well. Cook until the tomatoes turn soft.
3. Add the round gourd and cook covered on low heat. Mix well.
4. Serve hot, garnished with green chillies and coriander.

Sitafal Ki Sabzi

Fenugreek-flavoured pumpkin

Serves: 4-6

Ingredients:

Pumpkin (*sitafal*), diced into 1" cubes   1 kg
Mustard (*sarson*) oil   ½ cup / 85 ml
Fenugreek seeds (*methi dana*)   1 tsp / 3 gm
Coriander seeds (*sabut dhaniya*)   1 tsp / 2 gm
Whole red chillies (*sabut lal mirch*),
    roasted   4
Turmeric (*haldi*) powder   ½ tsp / 1 gm
Salt to taste
Red chilli powder   1 tsp / 1½ gm
Dry mango powder (*amchur*)   1 tbsp / 8 gm
Sugar   1 tsp / 3 gm

Method:

1. Heat the mustard oil in a wok (*kadhai*); add the fenugreek seeds, coriander seeds, whole red chillies and sauté till light brown.
2. Add the pumpkin and mix well. Stir in the turmeric powder, salt, red chilli powder, dry mango powder and sugar. Cook on low heat till the pumpkin is done.
3. Serve hot.

Gucchi Mattar

Morel mushrooms and green peas

Serves: 2-4

Ingredients:

Morel mushrooms (*gucchi*), soaked
   in warm water for 1 hour   100 gm
Green peas (*mattar*)   500 gm
Clarified butter (*ghee*)   2 tbsp / 30 gm
Onion, paste   1 cup / 300 gm
Garlic (*lasan*), paste   1 tbsp / 18 gm
Ginger (*adrak*), paste   1 tbsp / 18 gm
Tomato purée   1½ cups / 300 ml
Coriander (*dhaniya*) powder   3 tsp / 4½ gm
Red chilli powder   2 tsp / 3 gm
Cumin (*jeera*) powder   1 tsp / 3 gm
Garam masala powder (see p. 6) 3 tsp / 6 gm
Yoghurt (*dahi*)   1 cup / 180 gm
Asafoetida (*hing*)   ½ tsp / 1 gm
Salt to taste

Method:

1. Heat the clarified butter in a wok (*kadhai*); add the onion, garlic-ginger pastes and sauté till light brown in colour.
2. Add the tomato purée, coriander, red chilli, cumin, garam masala powders, yoghurt and asafoetida. Pour in 2 cups of water. Boil till the gravy thickens.
3. Then, add the mushrooms and green peas and cook till very little gravy remains and the clarified butter is seen on the surface.
4. Serve hot.

Punjabi Chana
Spicy chickpeas

Serves: 4-6

Ingredients:

Chickpeas (*kabuli chana*), soaked in
water for 2 hours, drained 1½ cups / 225 gm
Baking powder ½ tsp / 3 gm
Salt to taste
Clarified butter (*ghee*) ½ cup / 95 gm
Garlic (*lasan*), paste 6 tsp / 36 gm
Whole red chillies (*sabut lal mirch*),
ground with a little water 10
Coriander seeds (*sabut dhaniya*),
ground with a little water 6 tsp / 12 gm
Tomatoes, chopped 4 cups / 800 gm
Green chillies, slit 10
Ginger (*adrak*), finely chopped ¼ cup / 20 gm
Lemon (*nimbu*) juice 3 tbsp / 45 ml
Garam masala powder (see p. 6) 2 tsp / 4 gm

Method:

1. Boil the chickpeas in sufficient water with baking powder and salt until tender. Drain them and keep aside.
2. Heat the clarified butter in a pan; add the garlic paste and fry until golden. Add the whole red chilli and coriander seed pastes. Stir fry until the water evaporates.
3. Add the tomatoes, green chillies and ¾th of the ginger. Bring to a boil, reduce the heat and cook until the clarified butter comes to the surface.
4. Add the boiled chickpeas to the mixture. Cook for 5 minutes. Add the lemon juice and garam masala powder. Stir well.
5. Serve hot, garnished with the remaining ginger.

Ghia Ka Kofta
Bottle gourd dumplings in a tangy gravy

Serves: 2-4

Ingredients:

For the koftas:

Bottle gourd (*lauki*), peeled, grated, boiled for 5 minutes, drained	½ kg
Gram flour (*besan*)	½ cup / 50 gm
Green chillies, chopped	4
Ginger (*adrak*), 1" piece, finely chopped	1
Salt to taste	

Oil for frying

For the gravy:

Clarified butter (*ghee*)	½ cup / 95 gm
Onion, paste	1 cup / 300 gm
Garlic (*lasan*), paste	2 tsp / 12 gm
Ginger (*adrak*), paste	2 tsp / 12 gm
Tomato purée	1 cup / 200 ml
Coriander (*dhaniya*) powder	3 tsp / 4½ gm
Red chilli powder	2 tsp / 3 gm
Turmeric (*haldi*) powder	1 tsp / 1½ gm
Garam masala powder (see p. 6)	1 tsp / 2 gm
Yoghurt (*dahi*)	½ cup / 90 gm
Salt to taste	

Method:

1. For the koftas, combine all the ingredients in a bowl and mix well. Divide this mixture into equal lemon-sized portions and shape each portion into perfect rounds. Keep aside.

2. Heat the oil in a wok (*kadhai*); carefully slide in the koftas one at a time. Fry until golden brown. Remove them with a slotted spoon and drain the

excess oil on absorbent kitchen towels. Keep aside.

3. For the gravy, heat the clarified butter in a pan; add the onion, garlic and ginger pastes. Fry until light brown.

4. Add the tomato purée, coriander, red chilli, turmeric, garam masala powders, yoghurt and salt. Mix well.

5. Pour 2 cups of water and bring the mixture to a boil. Boil uncovered until the gravy thickens.

6. Add the fried koftas and cook for another 10 minutes on low heat. Serve hot.

≈

Milk for Gravy

*A cup of milk will work wonders with any gravy.
Besides improving the taste, it also makes
the gravy thicker and easier to digest.*

≈

Kadhi
Creamy yoghurt with gram flour dumplings

Serves: 4-6

Ingredients:

For the *pakoras*:

Gram flour (*besan*)	1 cup / 100 gm
Onions, chopped	½ cup / 120 gm
Ginger (*adrak*), chopped	1 tbsp / 25 gm
Green chillies, chopped	4-5
Salt	½ tsp / 2 gm
Baking powder	¼ tsp / 1½ gm

Oil for frying

For the *kadhi*:

Gram flour (*besan*)	1 cup / 100 gm
Yoghurt (*dahi*)	1 kg
Salt to taste	
Turmeric (*haldi*) powder	1 tsp / 1½ gm
Mustard oil	½ cup / 85 ml
Whole red chillies (*sabut lal mirch*)	10
Coriander seeds (*sabut dhaniya*)	1 tsp / 1½ gm
Fenugreek seeds (*methi dana*)	1 tsp / 3 gm
Mustard seeds (*rai*)	1 tsp / 3 gm
Cumin seeds (*sabut jeera*)	1 tsp / 2 gm
Asafoetida (*hing*)	¼ tsp / 1 gm
Curry leaves (*kadhi patta*)	15-20
For the tempering:	
Clarified butter (*ghee*)	2 tbsp / 30 gm
Red chilli powder	2 tsp / 3 gm

Method:

1. For the *pakoras*, to the gram flour, add onions, ginger, green chillies, salt and baking powder. Add

just enough water to make a thick batter. Divide the batter into lemon-sized balls and keep aside.

2. Heat the oil in a wok (*kadhai*); carefully slide in the balls and deep-fry till golden brown. Remove with a slotted spoon and drain the excess oil on absorbent kitchen towels. Keep aside.

3. For the *kadhi*, mix the gram flour with yoghurt. Add salt and turmeric powder.

4. Heat the mustard oil till it smokes; add the whole red chillies, coriander, fenugreek, mustard and cumin seeds. When they crackle, add asafoetida.

5. Now add the gram flour mixture and the curry leaves. Cook on low heat for 2 hours.

6. For the tempering, heat the clarified butter and remove from the heat. Add the red chilli powder and immediately, pour this to the above mixture. Add the dumplings and serve hot.

Chilli Cure

The burning sensation caused by handling chillies or chilli powder can be reduced considerably, if the affected parts are washed with sugar or tamarind.

Sukhi Urad Dal

Dry black gram

Serves: 2-4

Ingredients:

Split black gram (*urad dal*), washed, drained	1 cup / 200 gm
Turmeric (*haldi*) powder	1 tsp / 1½ gm
Salt to taste	
Clarified butter (*ghee*)	½ cup / 95 gm
Onions, chopped	½ cup / 120 gm
Garlic (*lasan*), finely chopped	3 tsp / 9 gm
Ginger (*adrak*), thinly sliced	4 tsp / 12 gm
Green chillies, finely chopped	6
Cumin seeds (*sabut jeera*)	1 tsp / 2 gm
Red chilli powder	1 tsp / 1½ gm
Asafoetida (*hing*)	¼ tsp / 1 gm
Tomatoes, chopped	2
Green coriander (*hara dhaniya*), chopped	2 tbsp / 8 gm

Method:

1. Boil the split black gram in 2 cups of water with turmeric powder and salt. Cook until it turns soft and a little water remains.
2. Heat the clarified butter in a wok (*kadhai*); add the onions, garlic, ginger and sauté till light brown. Add the green chillies, cumin seeds, red chilli powder, asafoetida, tomatoes and green coriander.
3. Cook for a few minutes till the tomatoes turn soft. Then add this mixture to the cooked split black gram and mix well.
4. Serve hot.

Lobia Tariwala

Black-eyed peas curry

Serves: 2-4

Ingredients:

Black-eyed peas (*lobia*)	1 cup / 170 gm
Turmeric (*haldi*) powder	1 tsp / 1½ gm
Salt to taste	
Asafoetida (*hing*)	¼ tsp / 1 gm
Clarified butter (*ghee*)	½ cup / 95 gm
Onions, chopped	½ cup / 120 gm
Garlic (*lasan*), chopped	2 tsp / 8 gm
Ginger (*adrak*), chopped	2 tsp / 16 gm
Whole red chillies (*sabut lal mirch*)	3
Tomatoes, chopped	½ cup / 100 gm
Coriander seeds (*sabut dhaniya*)	1 tsp / 2 gm
Red chilli powder	2 tsp / 3 gm
Cumin (*jeera*) powder	2 tsp / 3 gm
Coriander (*dhaniya*) powder	2 tsp / 3 gm
Garam masala powder (see p. 6)	1 tsp / 2 gm

Method:

1. Boil the black-eyed peas in a pressure cooker with turmeric powder, salt, asafoetida and 3 cups of water for 15-20 minutes.
2. Heat the clarified butter in a wok (*kadhai*); add the onions, garlic, ginger and whole red chillies. Sauté till light brown.
3. Add the tomatoes, coriander seeds, red chilli powder, cumin powder and coriander powder. Fry till the tomatoes turn soft.
4. Pour in the boiled black-eyed peas mixture with the water. Mix well.
5. Serve hot.

Chane Ki Dal
Bengal gram flavoured with tomatoes

Serves: 2-4

Ingredients:

Split Bengal gram (*chana dal*)	1 cup / 160 gm
Split black gram (*urad dal*)	½ cup / 100 gm
Black cardamoms (*bari elaichi*)	3
Turmeric (*haldi*) powder	1 tsp / 1½ gm
Asafoetida (*hing*)	¼ tsp / 1 gm
Salt to taste	
Clarified butter (*ghee*)	½ cup / 95 gm
Onions, chopped	½ cup / 120 gm
Garlic (*lasan*), chopped	2 tsp / 6 gm
Tomatoes, chopped	1 cup / 200 gm
Red chilli powder	2 tsp / 3 gm
Coriander (*dhaniya*) powder	2 tsp / 3 gm
Ginger (*adrak*), chopped	3 tsp / 25 gm
Cumin (*jeera*) powder	1 tsp / 3 gm
Garam masala powder (see p. 6)	1 tsp / 2 gm
Green chillies, chopped	5
Green coriander (*hara dhaniya*), chopped	2 tbsp / 10 gm

Method:

1. Boil the split Bengal gram and black gram in 3 cups of water with black cardamoms, turmeric powder, asafoetida and salt. Cook till tender. Keep aside.
2. Heat the clarified butter in a wok (*kadhai*); add the onions and garlic and fry till light brown.
3. Add the remaining ingredients (except green coriander). Cook till the tomatoes turn soft. Add this to the split Bengal gram mixture. Mix well.
4. Serve hot, garnished with green coriander.

Dal Moong-Masoor

Two-in-one dal

Serves: 2-4

Vegetarian

Ingredients:

Green gram (*moong dal*)	½ cup / 95 gm
Lentil (*masoor dal*)	½ cup / 80 gm
Turmeric (*haldi*) powder	1 tsp / 1½ gm
Salt to taste	
Clarified butter (*ghee*)	½ cup / 95 gm
Onions, chopped	½ cup / 120 gm
Garlic (*lasan*), chopped	2 tsp / 6 gm
Cumin seeds (*sabut jeera*)	1 tsp / 2 gm
Tomatoes, chopped	½ cup / 100 gm
Coriander (*dhaniya*) powder	2 tsp / 3 gm
Red chilli powder	1 tsp / 1½ gm
Green coriander (*hara dhaniya*), chopped	2 tbsp / 10 gm

Method:

1. Boil the green gram and lentil in 2 cups of water with turmeric powder and salt. Cook until tender. Keep aside.
2. Heat the clarified butter in a wok (*kadhai*); add the onions, garlic and cumin seeds. Fry till light brown.
3. Add the tomatoes, coriander powder, red chilli powder and sauté till the tomatoes turn soft. Add this to the cooked green gram mixture. Mix well.
4. Serve hot, garnished with green coriander.

Amritsari Dal
Split black gram flavoured with mint

Serves: 4-6

Ingredients:

Split black gram (*urad dal*), soaked for 1 hour	1 cup / 200 gm
Bengal gram (*chana dal*), soaked for 1 hour	½ cup / 80 gm
Salt to taste	
Ginger (*adrak*), chopped	2 tbsp / 36 gm
Garlic (*lasan*), chopped	2 tbsp / 25 gm
Unsalted butter	½ cup / 45 gm
Clarified butter (*ghee*)	½ cup / 95 gm
Onions, chopped	½ cup / 120 gm
Green chillies, chopped	6
Tomatoes, chopped	¼ cup / 50 gm
Mint (*pudina*) leaves	1 tbsp / 4 gm

Method:

1. Drain both the grams and cook in 5 cups of water in a large pan; add salt. Bring to a boil, reduce the heat and keep removing the scum that surfaces.
2. Add 1½ tbsp of ginger and garlic each and unsalted butter. Cook covered until the mixed gram is tender and a little water remains. Remove and mash the mixture against the sides of the pan with a large spoon.
3. Heat the clarified butter in a pan; add the onions and fry until light brown. Add the remaining ginger-garlic, green chillies, tomatoes and mint leaves. Cook until the tomatoes are mashed. Pour this into the above mixture and stir. Serve hot.

Gucchi Pulao
Morel mushrooms with rice

Serves: 2-4

Accompaniments

Ingredients:

Rice, cleaned, drained	1 cup / 200 gm
Morel mushrooms (*gucchi*), soaked in warm water for ½ hour, drained	50 gm
Clarified butter (*ghee*)	1 cup / 190 gm
Cinnamon (*dalchini*) sticks	2
Cloves (*laung*)	6
Green cardamoms (*choti elaichi*)	3
Black cumin (*shahi jeera*) seeds	1 tsp / 2 gm
Onions, chopped	½ cup / 60 gm
Salt to taste	
Water	2 cups / 400 ml

Method:

1. Heat the clarified butter in a wok (*kadhai*); add the cinnamon sticks, cloves, green cardamoms, black cumin seeds and onions. Sauté till the onions turn light brown. Add the rice and salt. Fry for 3 minutes.
2. Add the mushrooms and water. When the rice mixture comes to a boil, reduce the heat and cook covered till the rice is done and the water is absorbed.
3. Serve hot.

Tamatar Pulao
Tomato rice

Ingredients:

Rice, cleaned	2 cups / 400 gm
Clarified butter (*ghee*)	1 tbsp / 15 gm
Cumin seeds (*sabut jeera*)	1 tsp / 2 gm
Whole red chillies (*sabut lal mirch*)	4
Bay leaves (*tej patta*)	2-3
Onion, sliced	1
Salt	1½ tsp / 5 gm
Ginger (*adrak*), ground	1 tsp / 6 gm
Garlic (*lasan*), ground	1 tsp / 6 gm
Tomato paste	1 tbsp / 20 gm
Water	4 cups / 800 ml

Method:

1. Heat the clarified butter in a wok (*kadhai*); add the cumin seeds, whole red chillies and bay leaves. Sauté till light brown.
2. Add the onion, salt, ginger and garlic. Stir for 2-3 minutes.
3. Add the rice and mix well. Add the tomato paste. Fry for 5 minutes and then add the water.
4. When the rice mixture comes to a boil, reduce the heat and cook covered till the rice is done and the water is absorbed.
5. Serve hot.

Dal Ki Khichari

Mixed dals cooked with rice

Serves: 4-6

Ingredients:

Split green gram (*moong dal*)	½ cup / 95 gm
Split red gram (*arhar dal*)	½ cup / 80 gm
Lentil (*masoor dal*)	½ cup / 80 gm
Clarified butter (*ghee*)	1 tsp
Water	5 cups / 1 lt
Salt	3 tsp / 12 gm
Turmeric (*haldi*) powder	½ tsp / 1½ gm
Ginger-garlic (*adrak-lasan*), paste	1 tbsp / 12 gm
Rice, cleaned	4 cups / 800 gm

Method:

1. Heat the clarified butter in a wok (*kadhai*); add the first three ingredients and gently fry for 5-10 minutes.
2. Add 1½ cups of water and cook till all the water is absorbed and the dals are soft. Add the salt, turmeric powder, ginger-garlic paste and rice. Mix well.
3. Add the remaining water and cook on low heat until all the water is absorbed and the rice is done.
4. Serve hot.

Bhature
Deep-fried leavened bread

Serves: 4-6

Ingredients:

Refined flour (*maida*)	4 cups / 400 gm
Baking powder	1 tsp / 6 gm
Salt	1 tsp / 4 gm
Sugar	1 tsp / 3 gm
Yoghurt (*dahi*),	1 cup / 180 gm
Warm water	6 tbsp / 90 ml
Clarified butter (*ghee*)	1 tbsp / 15 gm
Oil for frying	

(See photograph on page 61)

Method:

1. Sieve the refined flour, baking powder and salt together. Add the sugar, yogurt and warm water to make a smooth dough. Grease your palms with 1 tbsp of oil and continue kneading till the dough becomes pliable. Cover with a moist cloth and keep aside for 2 hours.

2. Divide the dough into 12 lemon-sized balls. Roll them out into discs of 4″ diameter.

3. Heat the oil in a wok (*kadhai*); fry each disc until it puffs up. Turn and cook the other side too. Remove with a slotted spoon and drain the excess oil on absorbent kitchen towels.

4. Serve hot with Punjabi *chana* (see p. 60).

Sada Kulcha
Plain baked bread

Ingredients:

Milk	1 cup / 180 ml
Sugar	1 tsp / 6 gm
Yeast	3 tsp
Refined flour (*maida*)	4 cups / 400 gm
Salt	1 tsp / 3 gm
Clarified butter (*ghee*)	1 tbsp / 15 gm
Yoghurt (*dahi*)	4 tbsp / 120 gm
Water	½ cup / 100 ml
Poppy seeds (*khuskhus*)	2 tbsp / 18 gm

Method:

1. Warm the milk in a pan, add the sugar and yeast. Remove from the heat and leave aside to froth for 20 minutes.

2. Sieve the flour with salt. Pour the yeast mixture and clarified butter. Mix well. Slowly add the yoghurt and knead to make a soft dough. Cover with a moist cloth and leave aside for 6 hours.

3. Knead well again, if required, and add a little warm water. Divide the dough into 10 lemon-sized portions and roll them out into thick discs of 5″ diameter. Place them on a baking tray. Cover with a damp cloth for another 30 minutes to rise.

4. Brush the top with a little milk or clarified butter and sprinkle the poppy seeds.

5. Bake in a preheated oven for 10 minutes. Remove and shallow-fry on a griddle (*tawa*) with oil till golden.

Lachha Paratha
Layered unleavened fried bread

Serves: 4-6

Ingredients:

Refined flour (*maida*)	2 ⅓ cups / 230 gm
Salt to taste	
Milk	1¼ cups / 225 ml
Water	⅔ cup / 135 ml
Clarified butter (*ghee*)	¾ cup / 150 gm
Aniseed (*saunf*), crushed	2 tsp / 4 gm
Oil for shallow frying	

Method:

1. Sieve the refined flour and salt together. Add the milk and water and knead into a smooth dough. Add ⅓ of the clarified butter, melted, and the aniseed. Knead again to make the dough softer and smoother.
2. Divide the dough into 12 lemon-sized balls and roll out into 6″ discs. Pat 1 tsp of clarified butter evenly over one side. With a sharp knife, cut from the centre to the outside edge. Roll tightly, from the cut, all the way around so that it makes a neat cone. Stand the cone upright on its base and press it down into a patty. Similarly, work the remaining pieces of dough. Refrigerate them, covered, for an hour on a butter paper.
3. Roll out each patty into 6″ diameter.
4. Heat a griddle (*tawa*) and shallow-fry the patties on low heat until golden on both sides. Serve hot.

Tandoori Roti
Baked bread

Serves: 2-4

Ingredients:

Wholewheat flour (*atta*)	2½ cups / 250 gm
Salt to taste	
Clarified butter (*ghee*)	1 tbsp / 15 gm
Water	1½ cups / 300 ml

Method:

1. Sieve the wholewheat flour and salt together. Add the clarified butter and water, gradually, and knead well to make a soft dough. Cover with a moist cloth and keep aside for half an hour.
2. Divide the dough into 10 lemon-sized balls. Flatten each ball between the palms and roll each out to make *rotis* of about 5" diameter.
3. Bake the *rotis* in a preheated oven for 3 minutes till pale brown in colour.
4. Serve hot.

Missi Roti
Spicy gram flour bread

Serves: 2-4

Ingredients:

Gram flour (*besan*)	1½ cups / 150 gm
Refined flour (*maida*)	½ cup / 50 gm
Green chillies, chopped	5
Ginger (*adrak*), chopped	5 tsp / 15 gm
Green coriander (*hara dhaniya*), chopped	1 tbsp / 5 gm
Pomegranate seeds (*anardana*), crushed	4 tsp / 8 gm
Cumin seeds (*sabut jeera*), crushed	3 tsp / 6 gm
Nigella seeds (*kalongi*), crushed	5 tsp / 7½ gm
Salt	2 tsp / 9 gm
Clarified butter (*ghee*)	2 tbsp / 30 gm
Butter	½ cup / 85 gm

Method:

1. Mix both the flours together. Add the green chillies, ginger, green coriander, pomegranate seeds, cumin seeds, nigella seeds, salt and clarified butter. Mix well. Knead with enough water to make a smooth dough.
2. Divide the dough into 10 lemon-sized balls and roll them out to make *rotis* of 6″ diameter.
3. Heat the griddle (*tawa*) on medium heat and lay the *roti* flat on it. Cook on both sides until golden brown in colour. Remove from the griddle, smear with butter and serve.

Makkai Ki Roti

Maize flour bread

Serves: 2-4

Ingredients:

Maize flour (*makkai ka atta*) 1½ cups / 150 gm
Wholewheat flour (*atta*) ½ cup / 50 gm
Salt 1 tsp / 4 gm
Clarified butter (*ghee*) for frying

Method:

1. Sieve both the flours and the salt. Make a smooth dough with warm water and cover the dough with a moist cloth for 10 minutes.
2. Divide the dough into 8 lemon-sized portions and flatten them to form discs. Sprinkle them with flour and carefully roll them out to make *rotis* of 5″ diameter.
3. Heat the griddle (*tawa*) on medium heat and lay the *roti* flat on it.
4. Add a little clarified butter on the sides and fry. Turn the *roti* over and fry till golden brown.
5. Serve hot.

Kheer

Sweetened rice pudding

Desserts

Ingredients:

Basmati rice, soaked in water for
  30 minutes, drained   1 cup / 200 gm
Milk   11 cups / 2 lt
Green cardamoms (*elaichi*), cracked   5
Raisins (*kishmish*), soaked in water for
  30 minutes, drained   ½ cup / 60 gm
Condensed milk   2 cups / 440 gm
Almonds (*badam*), blanched,
  peeled, sliced   ½ cup / 65 gm

Method:

1. Bring the milk to a boil. Then add the green cardamoms and rice. Cook, stirring continuously, until the milk is fully absorbed and the rice is tender and broken.
2. Add the raisins and the condensed milk. Cook, stirring frequently, until the mixture obtains a thick consistency and sticks to the ladle.
3. Remove from the heat and transfer to a serving dish.
4. Garnish with almonds and serve chilled.

Phirni
Ground rice dessert

Ingredients:

Milk	3 cups / 540 ml
Rice, ground	3 tbsp
Sugar	6 tbsp / 75 gm
Green cardamom (*choti elaichi*) powder	½ tsp / 1 gm
Vetiver (*kewda*) essence	1 tbsp / 15 ml
Pistachios (*pista*), blanched, sliced	2 tbsp / 30 gm

Method:

1. Mix 4 tbsp of milk with the ground rice and make a smooth paste. Keep aside.
2. Bring the rest of the milk to a boil, add the sugar and stir until it dissolves completely. Remove it from the heat, mix in the ground rice paste and return to the heat. Stir constantly until the mixture thickens. Remove the pan from the heat. Add the green cardamom powder and vetiver essence; mix well.
3. Pour this mixture into individual dessert bowls and garnish with pistachios. Serve chilled.

Desserts

Shahi Tukda
Rich bread dessert sprinkled with dry fruits

Serves: 2-4

Ingredients:

Bread, slices cut into triangles,
with the crust removed — 4
Clarified butter (*ghee*) — 2 tsp / 10 gm
Milk, full-cream — 1½ cups / 270 ml
Sugar — 4 tbsp / 50 gm
Saffron (*kesar*), dissolved in
2 tbsp of hot water — a few strands
Almonds (*badam*), blanched,
peeled, sliced — 10
Raisins (*kishmish*), soaked in
hot water for 15 minutes — 10

Method:

1. Heat the oil and fry the bread triangles till golden in colour. Remove with a slotted spoon and drain on absorbent kitchen towels. Keep aside.

2. Heat the clarified butter in a large frying pan. Add the fried slices of bread. Pour the milk over them and sprinkle the sugar. Turn the slices over carefully, taking care that they do not break. Cook till the milk thickens and changes colour, stirring gently.

3. Remove from the heat, add the saffron and serve chilled sprinkled with almonds and raisins.

Sevain
Vermicelli milk pudding

Ingredients:

Vermicelli (*sevain*)	1¼ cups / 250 gm
Clarified butter (*ghee*)	½ cup / 95 gm
Cloves (*laung*)	10
Green cardamoms (*choti elaichi*), seeds	11
Milk	6 cups / 1080 ml
Brown sugar	¾ cup / 225 gm
Almonds (*badam*), chopped	½ cup / 65 gm
Raisins (*kishmish*)	¼ cup / 30 gm
Rose water (*gulab jal*)	3 tsp / 15 ml

Method:

1. Heat the clarified butter in a wok (*kadhai*); add the cloves and green cardamoms. Sauté well for 2-3 minutes to release their aromatic oils.
2. Add the vermicelli and fry for 2-3 minutes without breaking the strands. Add the milk and bring to a boil. Lower the heat, add the brown sugar and let it simmer, stirring gently until it dissolves. Cook for 15-20 minutes till the vermicelli becomes soft.
3. Mix the almonds and raisins and stir for another 5 minutes. Add the rose water. Stir till the mixture is thick, remove from the heat. Keep aside to cool.
4. Chill before serving.

Desserts

Mithe Pille Chawal

Sweetened yellow rice

Ingredients:

Rice, washed	2 cups / 400 gm
Clarified butter (*ghee*)	2 tsp / 10 gm
Cloves (*laung*)	4
Black cardamom (*bari elaichi*)	1
Water	4½ cups / 900 ml
Saffron (*kesar*) or yellow colour	a pinch
Sugar	1 cup / 200 gm

Method:

1. Heat the clarified butter in a wok (*kadhai*); add the cloves and black cardamom. Fry for 1-2 minutes.
2. Add the rice and mix well. Pour in the water and the saffron or edible colour. Cook until the rice is half done.
3. Mix the sugar and cook on low heat until all the water evaporates and the rice is tender. Serve hot.

Suji Ka Halwa
Semolina pudding

Desserts

Ingredients:

Semolina (*suji*)	1 cup / 200 gm
Clarified butter (*ghee*)	¾ cup / 140 gm
Sugar	1 cup / 200 gm
Milk	4 cups / 640 ml
Green cardamom (*choti elaichi*) powder	1 tsp / 5 gm
Almonds (*badam*)	¼ cup / 38 gm
Saffron (*kesar*)	a pinch

Method:

1. Heat the clarified butter in a wok (*kadhai*); add the semolina and fry on low heat till the colour changes to light brown.
2. Add the sugar, milk, green cardamom powder, almonds and saffron. Cook till the mixture becomes thick and the clarified butter shows on the surface.
3. Serve hot.

Gajrela
Carrot and milk pudding

Ingredients:

Carrots (*gajar*), scraped,
grated finely   1 kg
Milk   11 cups / 2 lt
Sugar   1½ cups / 300 gm
Clarified butter (*ghee*)   1 cup / 190 gm
Raisins (*kishmish*)   ½ cup / 60 gm
Almonds (*badam*), blanched,
peeled, sliced   ½ cup / 65 gm
Charoli seeds (*chironji*)   ½ cup / 50 gm

Method:

1. Boil the carrots in the milk, stirring frequently until the milk is completely absorbed.
2. Reduce the heat and add the sugar and clarified butter. Fry until the sugar is dissolved and the carrots turn deep red in colour. Mix in the raisins, almonds and charoli seeds.
3. Serve hot.

Suggested Menus

Non-vegetarian
Saag Meat *(Lamb cooked with spinach)*
Tandoori Murgh *(Grilled chicken)*

or

Vegetarian
Gobi Aloo *(Crispy cauliflower with potatoes)*
Punjabi Chana *(Spicy chickpeas)*

Accompaniments
Tandoori Roti *(Baked bread)*
Bhature *(Deep-fried leavened bread)*

Dessert
Kheer *(Sweetened rice pudding)*

Non-vegetarian
Murgh Makhani *(Chicken in a rich butter gravy)*
Amritsari Machchi *(Crispy fried fish)*

or

Vegetarian
Chane Ki Dal *(Bengal gram flavoured with tomatoes)*
Bharva Bhindi *(Stuffed okra)*

Accompaniments
Tamatar Pulao *(Tomato rice)*
Lachha Paratha *(Layered unleavened fried bread)*

Dessert
Gajrela *(Carrot and milk pudding)*

Glossary of Cooking Terms

Blanch — To immerse vegetables and meat briefly in boiling water.

Fritter — A portion of batter-coated food, deep-fried until crisp.

Marinate — To soak meat, fish or vegetable in a mixture of seasoning ingredients to add flavour and to make it tender.

Purée — To blend food in a blender or food processor to a smooth, thick mixture.

Sauté — To fry quickly over strong heat in oil or clarified butter.

Sieve — To shake a dry ingredient through a sieve or flour sifter, to remove lumps.

Simmer — To keep boiling or bubbling gently on a low flame.

Stir-fry — To cook over high heat with oil or clarified butter, stirring briskly.

Temper — To fry spices and flavourings in hot oil or clarified butter, and to pour this over the main preparation.

Index

ISBN: 81-7436-158-8

Fourth Impression
© **This edition Roli & Janssen BV 2007**
Published in India by Roli Books
in arrangement with Roli & Janssen BV
M-75, Greater Kailash-II Market,New Delhi-110 048, INDIA
Phones: ++91 (011) 29212782, 29212271, 29210886
Fax: ++91 (011) 29217185, E-mail: roli@vsnl.com
Website: rolibooks.com

Photographs: Dheeraj Paul

Printed and bound in Singapore